The Challenges of Storm Chasing

by Chris Downey

Editorial Offices: Glenview, Illinois • Parsippany, New Jersey • New York, New York
Sales Offices: Needham, Massachusetts • Duluth, Georgia • Glenview, Illinois
Coppell, Texas • Ontario, California • Mesa, Arizona

3 4 5 6 7 8 9 10 V0G1 14 13 12 11 10 09 08 07 06

The Most Powerful of All

The rain from thunderstorms provides water for Earth. Without that water, trees and plants wouldn't be able to grow and life wouldn't be able to exist. Thunderstorms also have negative aspects. They can often create strong winds, hail, and lightning. These things are dangerous and can cause much damage. However, thunderstorms create one type of weather that is more dangerous than all of those things: tornadoes.

Dangerous storms most often appear in the plains of the United States. This area is known as Tornado Alley. Tornado Alley has lots of dangerous storms because of weather patterns that occur in spring. This makes spring the best season to spot a tornado, which is a funnel-shaped cloud of spinning air.

A tornado can leave a path of **devastation** if it touches down where there are people and buildings. But as dangerous as tornadoes are, they are amazing to look at. A few brave and curious people known as storm chasers spend their time tracking and observing these storms.

Torna
Alle

Chase that storm!

Some storm chasers follow thunderstorms for scientific study, yet others do it purely for excitement. Many storm chasers are interested in weather patterns and meteorology. Meteorology is the study of the atmosphere. Very few people actually make a career of chasing storms. Many do it for the thrill of seeing a tornado and the pleasure of learning more about these amazing and powerful weather events.

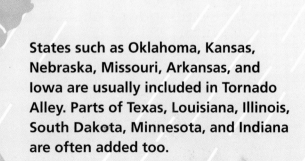

States such as Oklahoma, Kansas, Nebraska, Missouri, Arkansas, and Iowa are usually included in Tornado Alley. Parts of Texas, Louisiana, Illinois, South Dakota, Minnesota, and Indiana are often added too.

Thanks to TV shows and movies, many people think that storm chasing is constant action and excitement. They might be surprised to find out that real storm chasing is very different. In fact, one of the main challenges of chasing a storm is the long time spent waiting for a possible event. In a very good year, a chaser can expect a success rate of up to 10 percent. This means that 90 percent of the time is spent waiting and looking for storms. Many chases end up as busts, missions that don't result in the chaser seeing a large storm or tornado. A chaser must be very patient.

Even with help from weather reports and storm tracking equipment, a storm chaser must often make quick choices at a moment's notice. Some storm chasers use modern equipment to help forecast a storm's possible strength and direction. Satellites, radios, and laptop computers are important storm-tracking tools. Even with all of these aids, chasers are often faced with last-minute choices about when to stay put and when to move on to another location. This truck below has radar equipment that storm trackers can move from place to place to measure information about the storm at the site.

Modern equipment like laptop computers, video cameras, radios, and satellites help storm chasers learn where a storm may happen. This modern equipment also helps capture images of storms for others to see.

Chasers must be careful at all times. Not only is the weather dangerous, but many chasers carry expensive equipment to study the storms. This equipment isn't easy to replace, so chasers are very careful that it doesn't get damaged. They also pay close attention to their equipment. Those who do not can become victims to **thieving** people.

Some chasers take unnecessary risks in order to see a storm up close. Many seek out supercells. A supercell is a very powerful type of thunderstorm that can create tornadoes. Some chasers even go core punching. This is when a chaser drives through the center, or core, of a thunderstorm. The core of a storm has the most violent weather. Core punching is very dangerous. Many storm chasers refuse to do it, but it does give the closest view of any tornadoes that might form. Outside of the spinning core, areas of hail, heavy rain, and light rain travel around the supercell.

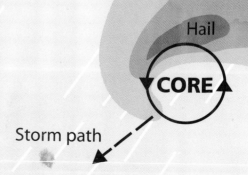

Heavy rain

Hail

CORE

Storm path

ght rain

The core is the area of a thunderstorm
where the most severe weather
occurs.

Tornadoes can do that?

A storm that may seem scary to you and me can look beautiful to a storm chaser. Even loud thunder claps may sound as soothing as a **lullaby** to a person who loves studying storms. However, this can be dangerous for storm chasers. They always have to remember that storms with lightning, driving rain, and very high winds are powerful natural events. The very same storms that chasers hope to see also threaten their lives.

High winds can flip the chaser's vehicle or blow out its windows. Heavy rain and hail can make it hard to see. Flooding and fog can make traveling harder and might strand a chaser in the path of a storm. A careful storm chaser knows to keep the car or truck in good shape and to watch the sky for any changes. Most important, a good storm chaser knows when to back off and seek safety. A **resourceful** chaser will plan an escape route from a dangerous storm before getting close to it.

Tornadoes form when a layer of cold air moves over a layer of warm air. The lighter air then rises up through the cold air. This creates a funnel cloud that rotates as the air masses change places.

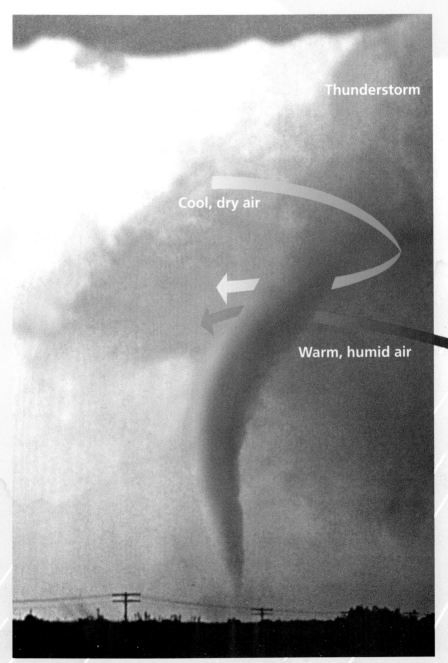

Thunderstorm

Cool, dry air

Warm, humid air

A tornado can have devastating effects on buildings, property, and land. A tornado with winds moving with furious speed will rip through a town and destroy everything in its path. Houses and mobile homes may be flattened, ripped apart, or carried away completely. A tornado can even peel the bark off trees! Such violence and destruction can occur at any time, as tornadoes touch down here and there without people being able to tell where and when.

On May 3, 1999, a series of tornadoes with wind speeds of more than three hundred miles per hour touched down in Oklahoma. The storms, which eventually turned north into Kansas, destroyed some houses and neighborhoods around Oklahoma City.

Tornadoes never approach **daintily.** You can hear them coming. Their winds make a very loud roar that many people compare to the sound of a train. Many towns have special sirens that will sound a warning when a tornado is approaching.

Tornadoes can generate winds of more than three hundred miles per hour. Such powerful winds can completely destroy buildings.

When Lightning Strikes

One of the biggest dangers for storm chasers is lightning. Lightning is a release of electricity in the atmosphere. Some lightning travels from clouds to the ground when it strikes. These strikes, also called lightning bolts, look like **veins** of light. Another form of lightning looks like a bright flash.

Lightning is a real threat to storm chasers. It can strike without warning and with deadly consequences. Nearly one hundred people are killed by lightning each year in the United States.

No one can be completely safe from lightning. Still, we can all use common sense in order to reduce our risk of being hurt by lightning strikes. The safest place to be when lightning strikes is inside a building. If you have to be outside during a lightning storm, stay close to the ground. Keep away from high places and avoid being near tall objects such as trees, telephone poles, or power lines. Lightning is more likely to either strike tall objects directly, or hit very close to them.

The Doppler on Wheels can be parked in the path of a storm so it can gather information while people are safely out of the way.

It All Began . . .

People started chasing storms for fun in the early 1950s. Roger Jensen, a native of North Dakota, was one of the first people to follow storms for fun and to photograph what he saw. Scientist Neil Ward, a respected tornado researcher, was also one of the pioneers of storm chasing. Ward was one of the first storm chasers to apply his observations to science. He was able to forecast weather changes based on information recorded while storm chasing.

In the 1960s, the U.S. government **constructed** the National Severe Storms Laboratory (NSSL) in Norman, Oklahoma. The NSSL studies storms and works to improve severe weather forecasting. Using modern technology and specially constructed equipment, scientists there work to collect data about storms.

One type of modern technology that the scientists in Norman use is termed the "Doppler on Wheels." It is a set of trucks carrying portable Doppler radar units. Doppler radar is usually used by local meteorologists to track weather changes, but the Doppler on Wheels is made for a different job. Trucks that carry the radar units are able to drive very close to tornadoes and gather data about how they form.

And they're off!

At one time, only weather scientists chased storms. Now all kinds of people are doing it, including thrill-seekers and people who like being around dangerous situations. With more chasers on the move, there are many more "chaser convergences" than ever before. A chaser convergence is when a group of chasers meets in a safe place on a chase day. Another group, similar to a chaser convergence, is a chase crowd. A chase crowd is a large group of chasers who stop on open roads to watch a storm. These crowds gather in places that are not safe from storms. By doing so, they make storm chasing even more dangerous.

People who want to get into storm chasing can now go on guided tours. These tours are led by experienced storm chasers who already know the ropes and will stay safe.

Storm chasing is becoming so widespread that storm tour groups have formed to cash in on its popularity. These groups charge people for the chance to chase storms with a tornado expert. Most of these tour groups operate in a safe, professional manner. But some of them are run recklessly enough that they cause people to question whether they should be allowed.

Obviously, it is important that storm-chasing tour groups be conducted by responsible people who know the dangers involved. Not surprisingly, people who study storms, such as meteorologists, generally make the best storm chasers. Meteorologists know more about what a storm is likely to do, and because of this knowledge they are able to chase storms with greater safety and efficiency. For instance, instead of driving through bad weather to reach a storm in progress, many meteorologists can position themselves to catch a storm that is forming.

How do they do it?

Good storm chasers know how to reduce their risk of getting hurt. They plan out their chase ahead of time, using maps and weather reports. Good storm chasers also make sure that the car or truck that they use is in good condition. They drive carefully and stay alert, avoiding slick or flooded areas. At the first sign of lightning or very strong winds, a good storm chaser knows to seek shelter and not put himself or herself in danger.

Storm chasers face many challenges. In addition to unpredictable weather, they must also contend with crowded roads and the growing number of fellow chasers. Still, many storm chasers feel that the rewards outweigh the risks. Some of the lucky ones are able to get as close to a storm as any human has ever been. Their bravery, in combination with modern technology, gives us a better understanding of how dangerous storms work!

Maps and compasses are among the many tools that good storm chasers use in order to plan the best and safest storm-chasing routes.

Glossary

branded *v.* marked by burning.

constructed *v.* put together.

daintily *adv.* with delicate beauty.

devastation *n.* the act of laying waste, destroying.

lullaby *n.* soft song sung to put a baby to sleep.

pitch *n.* a thick, black, sticky substance made from tar.

resourceful *adj.* good at thinking of ways to do things.

thieving *adj.* likely to steal.

veins *n.* natural channels through which water flows, or the tubes that carry blood through your body.